Artful Quotes

Coloring Book

Lindsey Boylan

The mind is everything. What you think you become.

—Buddha

DOVER PUBLICATIONS, INC.
Mineola, New York

A perfect blend of nature-inspired art and motivational quotations, this collection of 63 beautiful images is specially designed for the sophisticated colorist. Uplifting sayings and famous quotes, framed by pretty floral arrangements and abstract animal designs, will be sure to give cause for reflection. The pages in this deluxe edition are perforated and printed on one side only for easy removal and display.

Bibliographical Note
Artful Quotes Coloring Book is a new work, first published by Dover Publications, Inc., in 2016.

International Standard Book Number
ISBN-13: 978-0-486-80885-7
ISBN-10: 0-486-80885-8

Manufactured in the United States by RR Donnelley
80885801   2016
www.doverpublications.com

Nature
does nothing
in vain.

—Aristotle

Shine like the whole universe is yours.

—Rumi

Music
in the soul
can be heard
by the
universe.

—Lao Tzu

To be yourself
in a world
that is constantly
trying to make
you something else
is the greatest
accomplishment.

—Ralph Waldo Emerson

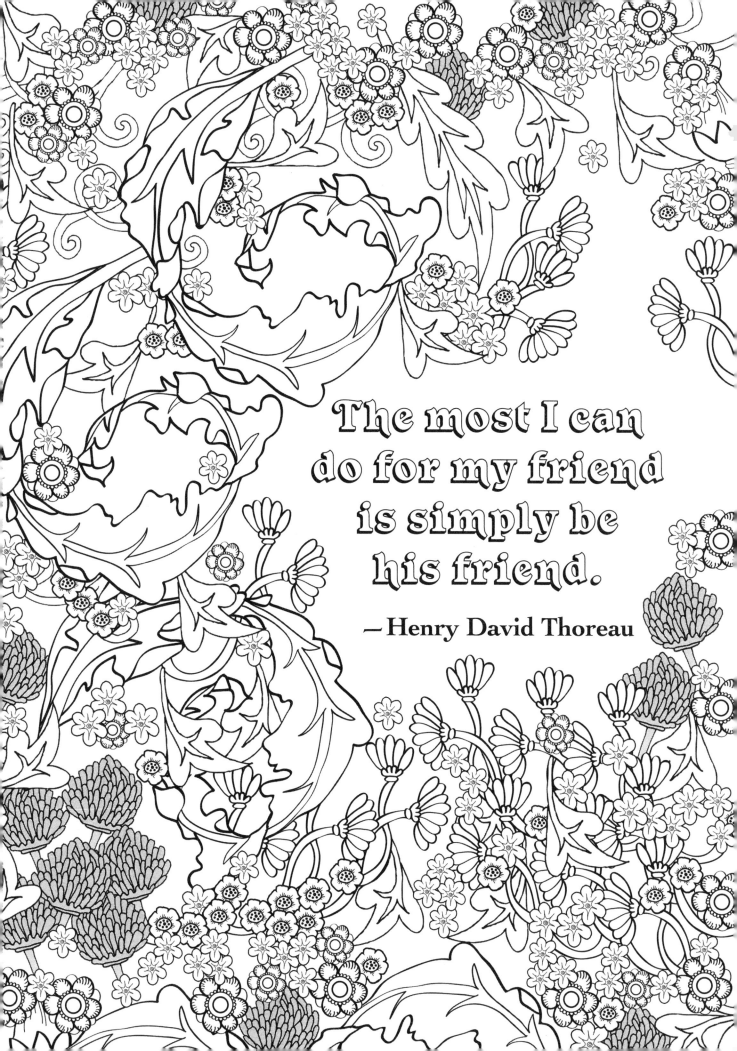

The most I can do for my friend is simply be his friend.

—Henry David Thoreau

In the end,
it's not the
years in your
life that count.
It's the life
in your years.

—Abraham Lincoln

Love
many things,
for therein lies
the true strength, and
whosoever loves much
performs much, and
can accomplish much,
and what is
done in love
is done well.

— Vincent van Gogh

Try to be a rainbow in someone's cloud.

—Maya Angelou

Nature does not hurry, yet everything is accomplished.

—Lao Tzu

Every great dream begins with a dreamer.

— Harriet Tubman

Change your thoughts and you change your world.

—Norman Vincent Peale

The secret
of getting
ahead
is getting
started.
—Mark Twain

The earth
laughs in
flowers.

—Ralph Waldo Emerson

Start
by doing
what's necessary;
then do what's
possible;
and suddenly
you are doing
the impossible.

—Saint Francis of Assisi

Since love grows within you, so beauty grows. For love is the beauty of the soul.

—Saint Augustine

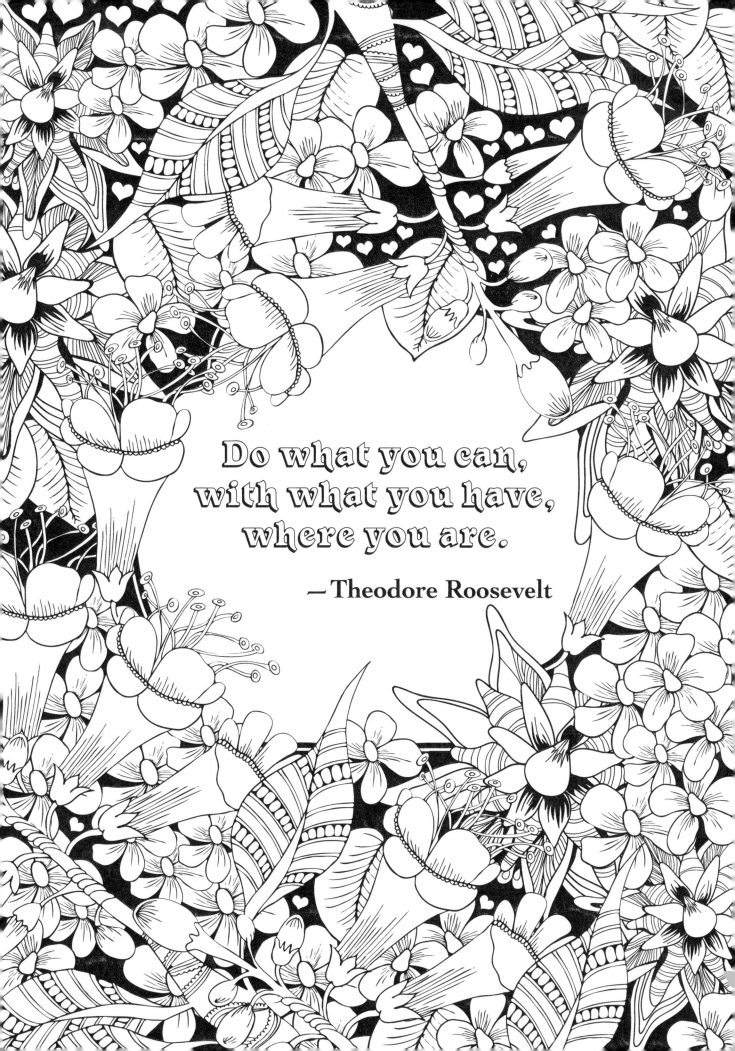

Do what you can,
with what you have,
where you are.

— Theodore Roosevelt

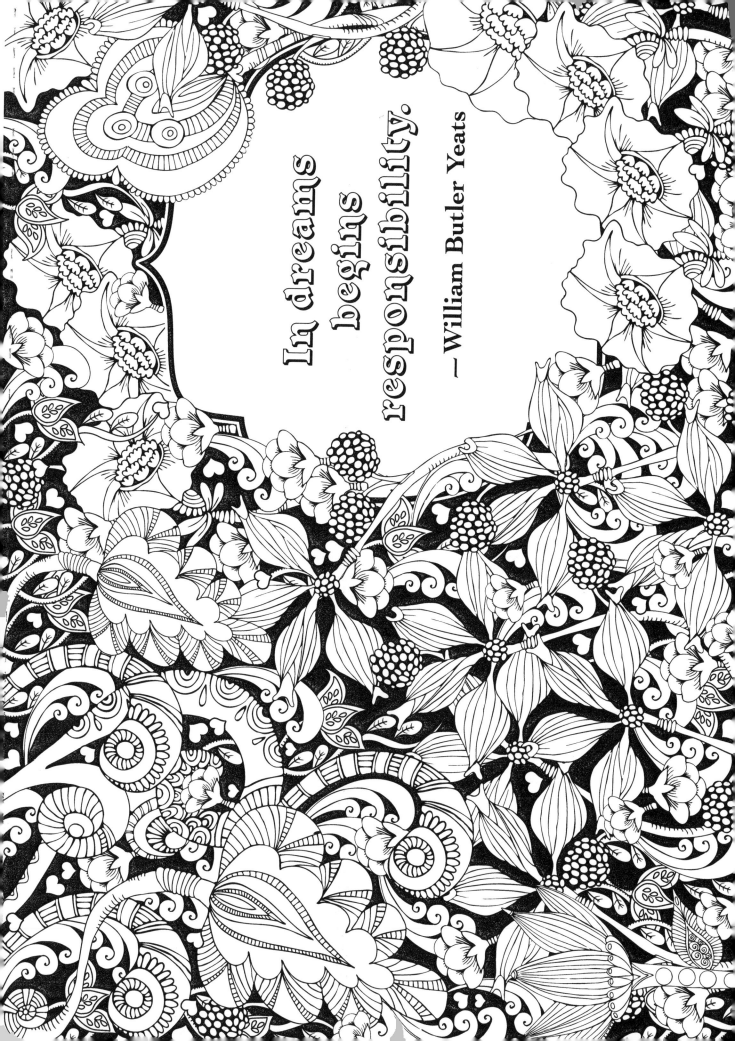

In dreams begins responsibility.

—William Butler Yeats

Do not
lose courage in
considering
your own
imperfections.

— Saint Francis de Sales

Simplicity, patience, compassion. These three are your greatest treasures.

—Lao Tzu

The only real
failure in life
is not to
be true
to the best
one knows.

—Buddha

The future belongs to those who believe in the beauty of their dreams.

— Eleanor Roosevelt

A thing of
beauty is
a joy forever.

—John Keats

Re-examine all that you have been told . . . dismiss that which insults your soul.

—Walt Whitman

When I let go
of what I am,
I become
what I
might be.

—Lao Tzu

Good actions
give strength
to ourselves and
inspire good actions
in others.
~Samuel Smiles

Keep your face to the sunshine and you cannot see a shadow.

—Helen Keller

Wherever you go, go with all your heart.

—Confucius

To have
courage for
whatever comes
in life—everything
lies in that.

—Saint Teresa of Avila

Forgiveness is the fragrance that the violet sheds on the heel that has crushed it.

—Mark Twain

All action results from thought, so it is thoughts that matter.

—Sai Baba

Even if I knew that tomorrow the world would go to pieces, I would still plant my apple tree.

—Martin Luther

Patience is
necessary,
and one cannot
reap immediately
where one
has sown.
—Soren Kierkegaard

Each person must live their life as a model for others.

—Rosa Parks

No one saves
us but ourselves.
No one can and
no one may. We
ourselves must
walk the path.

—Buddha

I find hope in the darkest of days, and focus in the brightest. I do not judge the universe.
—Dalai Lama

Beauty
surrounds us,
but usually we need
to be walking
in a garden
to know it.

—Rumi

You cannot do a kindness too soon, for you never know how soon it will be too late.

— Ralph Waldo Emerson

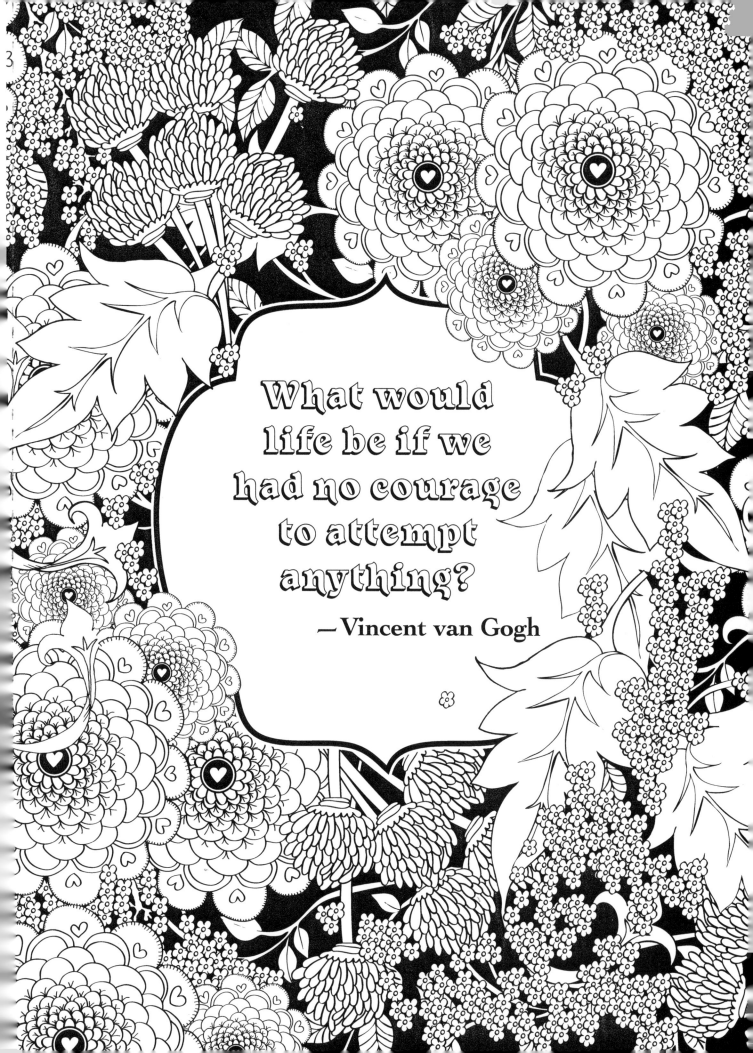

In all chaos there is a cosmos, in all disorder a secret order.

—Carl Jung

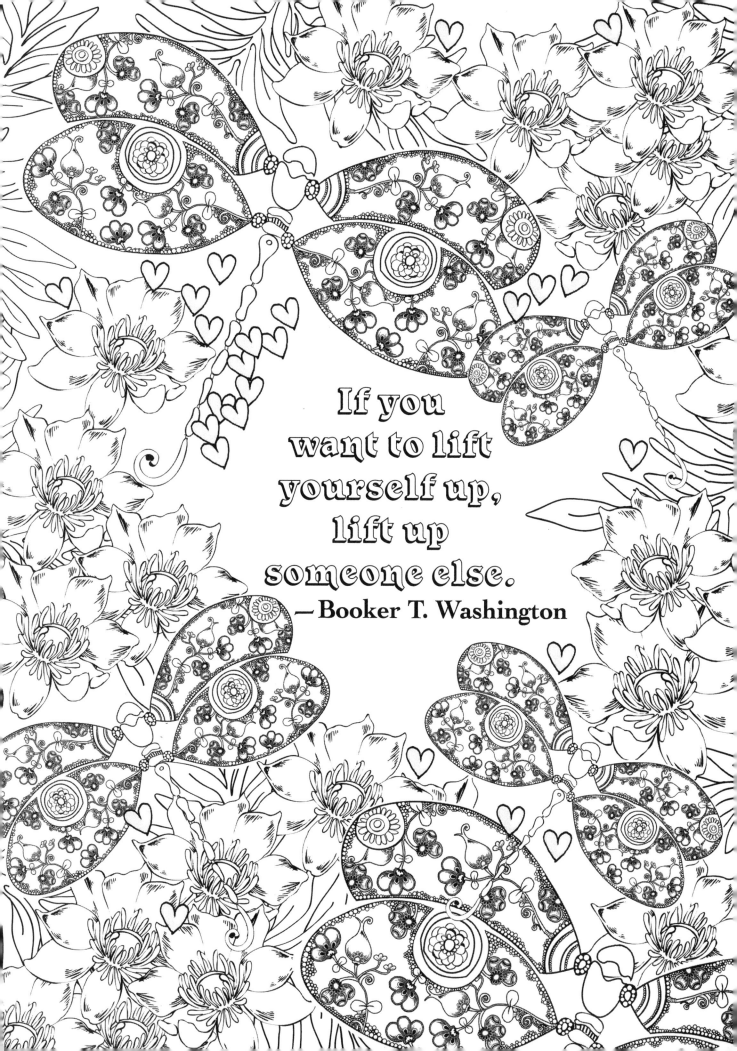

If you
want to lift
yourself up,
lift up
someone else.
— Booker T. Washington

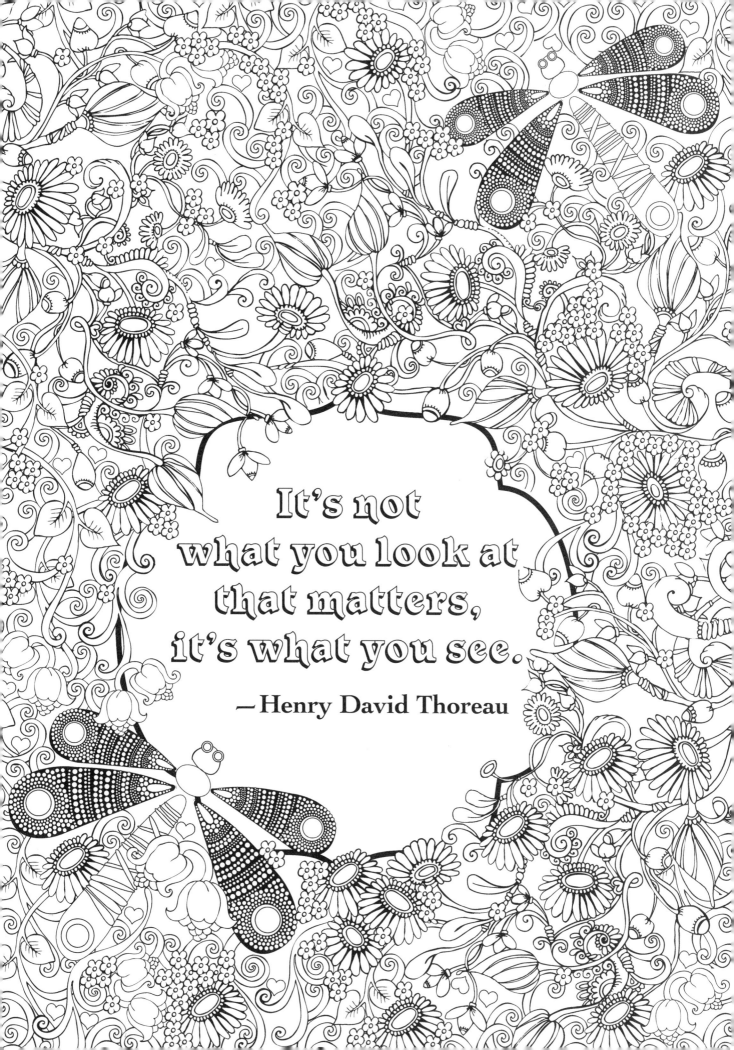

It's not
what you look at
that matters,
it's what you see.

—Henry David Thoreau

Kindness
is the language
which the deaf
can hear and the
blind can see.

—Mark Twain

Faith
is to believe
what you do not
see; the reward of
this faith
is to see
what you believe.

—Saint Augustine

You will never do anything in this world without courage. It is the greatest quality of the mind next to honor.

—Aristotle

It is never too late to be what you might have been.
—George Eliot

Life is not a problem to be solved, but a reality to be experienced.

—Soren Kierkegaard

Great things are done by a series of small things brought together.

—Vincent van Gogh

Light tomorrow with today.

—Elizabeth Barrett Browning

Life is a song—
sing it.
Life is a game—
play it.
Life is a
challenge—
meet it.
Life is a dream—
realize it.
Life is a
sacrifice—
offer it.
Life is love—
enjoy it.

—Sai Baba

The best
way to know God
is to love
many things.

— Vincent van Gogh

The art
of knowing
is
knowing
what to
ignore.

— Rumi

For it is in giving that we receive . . .

— Saint Francis of Assisi

Forever is composed of nows.

—Emily Dickinson

A loving
heart is the
truest wisdom.

—Charles Dickens

Everything has beauty, but not everyone sees it.

—Confucius

Your vision will become clear only when you can look into your own heart.

—Carl Jung

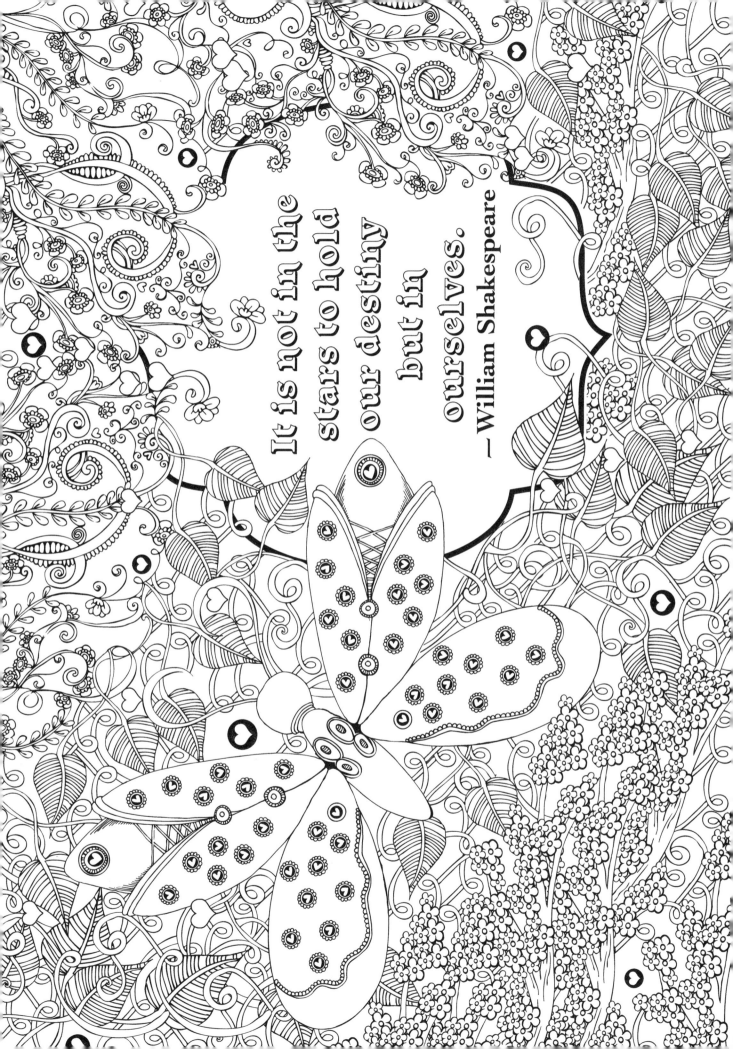

Live life as if
everything is
rigged in
your favor.

— Rumi